21st Century
Skills Library

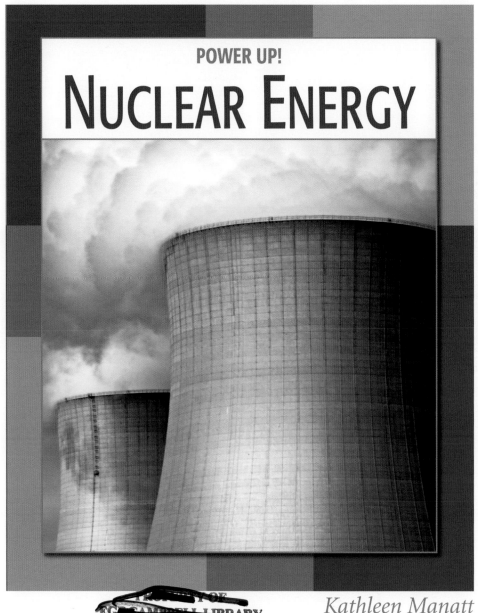

POWER UP!

NUCLEAR ENERGY

Kathleen Manatt

Cherry Lake Publishing
Ann Arbor, Michigan

Published in the United States of America by Cherry Lake Publishing
Ann Arbor, MI
www.cherrylakepublishing.com

Photo Credits: Page 2, © Rafael Rigues/StockXchange; Page 8, Photo Courtesy of Library of Congress; Page 12, Photo Courtesy of Library of Congress; Page 14, © MIYOKO OYASHIKI/CORBIS SYGMA; Page 15, Photo Courtesy of U.S. Department of Energy; Page 19, © Igor Kostin/Sygma/Corbis; Page 22, Photo Courtesy of Keith Adams; Page 24, © Marco Bulgarelli/Corbis; Page 29, © John Pilge/StockXchange

Library of Congress Cataloging-in-Publication Data
Manatt, Kathleen G.
  Nuclear energy / by Kathleen Manatt.
     p. cm. — (Power up!)
  Includes bibliographical references and index.
  ISBN-13: 978-1-60279-047-6 (lib. bdg.)   978-1-60279-099-5 (pbk.)
  ISBN-10: 1-60279-047-7 (lib. bdg.)   1-60279-099-X (pbk.)
  1. Nuclear energy—Juvenile literature. I. Title. II. Series.
  TK9148.M325 2008
  621.48—dc22   2007005655

*Cherry Lake Publishing would like to acknowledge the work of
The Partnership for 21st Century Skills.
Please visit www.21stcenturyskills.org for more information.*

TABLE OF CONTENTS

CHAPTER ONE

POWER FOR THE WORLD

*As more and more demands are made on the power
supply, cities experience occasional blackouts*

Have you ever had the electricity suddenly go off at night? There are no

lights, no TV, no video games, no computers. You look outside and see that

all your neighbors' houses are dark, too.

Suddenly the lights all come back on. The house is bright and noisy again, as if all the things that use electricity were turned on at once. Reliable electricity sure is important to our lives!

Electricity is created when magnets are spun around inside a giant coil of wires. The magnets and wires are the main parts of an electrical generator.

Spinning the magnets around can be done in many ways. Fast moving water can spin them. Burning coal and oil fuels can heat water to make steam. Then the steam can turn the magnets. The steam can also be made with another fuel: **atoms,** some of the smallest things in the universe.

Learning & Innovation Skills

Burning coal and oil often produces large amounts of air pollution. Many places around the world are trying to cut down on this pollution. However, huge amounts of electricity still are needed to provide power to every house, apartment, and business in the world. Think of 15 things in your home that use electricity. What could you do without?

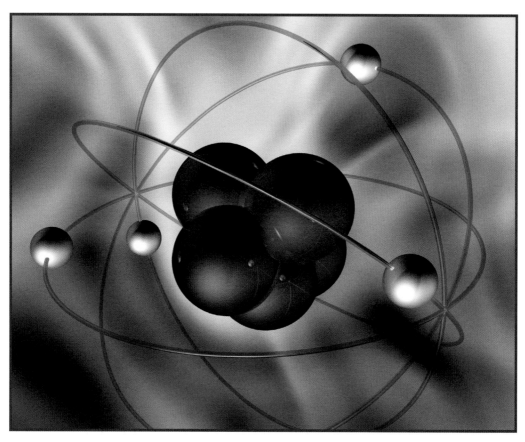

*Atoms are very, very tiny. In fact, a human hair
is about 1 million atoms wide.*

Everything in the world is made up of atoms. They are so small that it

takes a very powerful microscope to see them. However, even atoms can

be broken into parts. In the center of an atom is its **nucleus,** or core. Each

nucleus is made up of **protons** and **neutrons** that are clustered together.

Electrons spin around the nucleus. Amazingly, it takes a huge amount of energy to hold each tiny atom together.

The atoms we use for energy come from **uranium,** which is found in some rocks. The rocks are processed to get the uranium. Then it is formed into pellets. When enough pellets are put close together, they start forming a **chain reaction**. The atoms start splitting and creating heat. The heat is used to make steam to drive an electrical generator. However, when atoms are split, they also create **radiation,** which can harm living things or even kill them.

CHAPTER TWO

SMALL THINGS CAN BE MIGHTY

The U.S. dropped an atomic bomb on Nagasaki, Japan, on August 9, 1945. The north side of the city was destroyed.

During World War II, the United States raced to make an atomic bomb.

The U.S. feared the Nazis might make one first. But by the time the bomb

was made, the war in Europe was over. However, the war with Japan seemed like it would take a long time and many lives to win. To end the war quickly, the United States dropped atomic bombs on two Japanese cities. The war was over very soon afterward.

Peaceful Uses

Although nuclear energy can be used to destroy things, it has other uses, too. It can be harnessed to create electricity. The world's first nuclear power plant began producing power in 1954. It produced a tiny 5 megawatts, and the plant was in the Soviet Union. The United States' first nuclear power plant was in Shippingport, Pennsylvania. It began operation in 1957 and was closed down in 1982.

Learning & Innovation Skills

The Soviet plant was in the tiny town of Obninsk, about 60 miles south of the capital city of Moscow. Why do you think the news that the Soviet Union had the first nuclear power plant shook Americans? *Hint*: Think about the Cold War.

Nuclear power was also soon tried for several other types of projects. Ships were one of them. In 1954, the United States launched the world's first nuclear-powered submarine. It was called the *USS Nautilus.* In its 25 years of use, the *Nautilus* traveled almost half a million miles, much of it totally under water. Today the *Nautilus* is a museum on the Thames River in Groton, Connecticut.

Amazingly, some common medical machines use nuclear energy, too. One of these is the positron emission tomography (PET) scanning machine. It can take pictures of the inside of patients from the outside. Obviously, this is a big help to both doctors

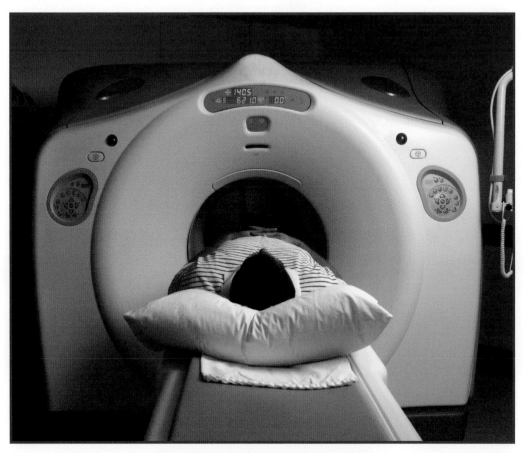

*For a PET scan, the patient lies on a long
table that slides into the machine.*

and patients. Doctors use PET scans to find cancer, study the brain, and

check the heart. PET scanners are wonderful but also *very* expensive. Each

one costs millions of dollars and must be run by specially trained staff.

CHAPTER THREE

DANGER!

Marie Curie received two Nobel Prizes for her work. She lived in Poland and France and is greatly honored in both nations.

Nuclear energy has been killing scientists since they first began experimenting with it. The famous Marie Curie died from effects of the radiation she worked with for decades. Just as World War II was ending in 1945, one of the American scientists working on the atomic bomb was killed. Harry Daghlian accidentally brought together two radioactive pieces. They began to heat, and Daghlian instinctively knocked them apart with his hand. He died three weeks later.

Nuclear Plant Disasters

Nuclear energy is powerful but also quite dangerous. There have been several minor accidents. Accidents occurred in Canada in 1952 and 1957. In the 1960s, accidents happened in Monroe, Michigan, and in Scotland, Switzerland, and Sweden. Serious accidents have also happened in Japan, Argentina, Germany, Spain, Hungary, and England. However, by far the two most serious accidents occurred at Three Mile Island in Pennsylvania and at Chernobyl in the former Soviet Union.

21st Century Content

Several world nations now get a majority of their electricity from nuclear energy. Nuclear electricity accounts for more than three-quarters of all electricity generated in France and Lithuania, and more than half of the total in Belgium, Sweden, and Slovakia.

A nuclear accident at Tokaimura, Japan, in 1999 meant everyone nearby had to be individually checked for radiation problems.

Three Mile Island is a huge nuclear energy plant in Pennsylvania. In 1979, it had two nuclear reactors. Three Mile Island was such a big plant that it produced nearly1,000 megawatt hours of electricity per hour. Most plants produced only 100 megawatts.

*Despite the accident in 1979, the Three Mile Island
nuclear plant is still in use today.*

On March 28, 1979, reactor No.1 was shut down. However, at exactly 4 A.M., the water pump failed on reactor No. 2. Then a pressure valve opened and should have closed, but it did not. More problems piled up quickly.

As a result, the nuclear reactor could not be chilled enough. So much heat built up that the nuclear fuel pellets began to melt. A melt of the reactor core is the most serious type of accident. Pregnant women and young children were evacuated from nearby homes. More problems occurred. A large, dangerous gas bubble built up in the plant. It was not until April 1 that the crisis passed.

As at all such plants, the Three Mile Island reactor was built inside a very strong cement building. It prevented the spread of radioactive material to the outside environment. However, some radioactive gas had to be allowed to escape to prevent a bigger explosion.

People all over the nation were deeply concerned. The No. 2 reactor was permanently shut down after the crisis passed. However, this took years to accomplish, and full-time monitoring goes on.

Learning & Innovation Skills

President Carter told the FBI to investigate the accident to see if the crisis at Three Mile Island had been caused deliberately. Who was the major enemy of the United States in 1979 when the accident occurred? *Hint*: Think about the Cold War.

A Much More Deadly Accident

In 1986, Chernobyl was a very large nuclear plant. It sits about 80 miles from the city of Kiev, in what was then the Soviet Union. In the early, early morning of April 26, some technicians at the plant decided to run a safety test. In doing the test, they purposely did not follow the safety precautions. It was a horrible mistake.

Explosions began at 1:23 A.M. They produced 200 times more radioactive particles than both the atomic bombs that fell on Japan. Soon a huge, huge fire blew the lid off the heavy steel and concrete building and carried it into the sky. The fire and smoke contained

Much of Chernobyl was totally destroyed in the 1986 accident and gave off huge amounts of deadly radiation.

not only radioactive particles but also rubble from the reactor. The fireball carried these into the air. Firefighters were called in, but it was an almost impossible task. The fire raged on.

The secretive Soviet government did not tell the world—or even its own people—about the accident. However, clouds of radiation began to drift over Europe. Then, on April 27, workers at a nuclear plant several hundred miles away in Sweden were found to have radiation particles on their clothing. Soon radiation was being detected throughout Europe and even the United States. Eventually radiation from Chernobyl contaminated nearly every country in the Northern Hemisphere.

Several dozen of the early firefighters died of radiation poisoning. They did not have the proper equipment and at the beginning did not even know about the radiation danger. Brave helicopter pilots tried to drop sand on the fire to put it out since water will not extinguish a radiation fire. The pilots put extra sheets of steel in the bottoms of their helicopters to protect themselves from radiation. It didn't work. They died, too.

21st Century Content

Radiation poisoning is a relatively new disease because it only began to occur after humans learned how to create nuclear energy. The disease causes vomiting, skin burns, weakness, fainting, and bleeding from the nose and mouth, among other things. Scientists continue to work to prevent the illness.

The abandoned radioactive town of Prypiat is only about
62 miles (100 km) from Ukraine's capital city of Kiev.

The town of Prypiat was just two miles from Chernobyl. Prypiat's

50,000 people, along with about 250,000 others, had to leave forever.

Their clothes, toys, sofas, pictures—everything — were and had to be

abandoned. Prypiat will not be safe for humans for several hundred years.

Over time and with enormous effort, the Chernobyl fire was put out.

The damaged reactor was buried forever in tons and tons and tons of cement to keep the remaining radiation in. But the damage was done.

In a few years, the rate of cancer in children from the Chernobyl area shot up 800 percent. Thousands of more people are expected to have cancer in the future because of their exposure to Chernobyl's radiation.

Because of the nuclear accidents of the past, people are aware of the dangers of nuclear energy. What are some safeguards that are important for people who live or work near a nuclear power plant?

*Children in Ukraine and elsewhere who were born well after the
accident are coming down with thyroid cancer and leukemia.*

Deformed insects were found in nearby countries. Some had four

legs on one side and none on the other. Others had bodies that were too

small and heads that were too big. Some had no eyes. Scientists say the

deformities were caused by radiation.

CHAPTER FOUR

A Nuclear-Powered Future

*Concern about nuclear energy has caused some plants
to be abandoned before completion.*

The accident at Three Mile Island caused Americans to slow down

their plans for more nuclear plants. People were frightened and began to

wonder if nuclear energy was really worth all the trouble. As a result, no new reactors have been built in the United States since then. However,

President George Bush began pushing for more nuclear plants in 2005.

Such plants would help free the United States from dependence on

foreign oil.

Every year, we create tons of radioactive waste that must be safely stored for many, many years.

Another problem is what to do with the uranium pellets once they are used up. They still contain dangerous radiation, and they must be stored for many, many years in safe places away from all human contact. The federal government has spent billions of dollars to build a waste site at Yucca Mountain in Nevada. However, it won't be ready until 2017.

We must address other issues about nuclear energy, too. The plants are more expensive to build than are those that use coal or oil. However, nuclear plants use less fuel than coal and oil ones do, so over time they can generate cheaper electricity. In addition, nuclear plants don't regularly cause air

Air pollution and global warming are two of the world's biggest problems today. How could you personally cut down on energy use to help solve these problems? Think of things you could do, such as riding your bike instead of riding in the car.

Why might Yucca Mountain be a good place to keep dangerous nuclear waste? *Hint*: Think about the population of Nevada.

pollution, while burning oil and coal does. This

pollution adds to the problem of global warming.

Decisions, Decisions, Decisions

There are many decisions we must make about

nuclear power in the future. We need to make

nuclear material safe, both when it is being used and

afterward. Right now, nuclear waste is being stored

around the country. The Yucca Mountain storage site

will not be ready for many years. Nor is there even

widespread agreement that Yucca Mountain is a good

place to keep nuclear waste.

Engineers today are designing safer plants. The

plants use simpler systems and have fewer parts, so

less can go wrong. However, it takes many years to build even one plant, and our energy needs are rising right now. Another problem is the supply of uranium. It will run out eventually. What new source will we use for nuclear energy? And where will future plants be built? Do you want one near you? These and other decisions lie in your future.

Several American cities, including Berkeley, California, and Tacoma Park, Maryland, have voted to become nuclear free zones.

GLOSSARY

atoms (AT-uhmz) very tiny material units that are the source of nuclear energy

chain reaction (cheyn ree-AK-shuhn) self-sustaining series of actions in which the release of neutrons from the splitting of one atom leads to the splitting of others

contaminated (kuhn-TAM-uh-neyt-ed) exposed to or filled with radiation

electrons (i-LEK-tronz) negatively charged parts of atoms

neutrons (NOO-tronz) electrically neutral parts of atoms

nucleus (NOO-klee-uhs) positively charged central portion of an atom, made up of neutrons and protons

protons (PROH-tonz) positively charged parts of atoms

radiation (rey-dee-EY-shuhn) stream of particles or electromagnetic waves given off by atoms of a radioactive substance

radiation poisoning (rey-dee-EY-shuhn POI-zuh-ning) severe and often fatal illness caused by contact with too much radiation

uranium (yoo-REY-nee-uhm) a heavy, toxic, silvery-white substance that is used to produce nuclear energy

FOR MORE INFORMATION

Books

Barron, Rachel Stiffler. *Lise Meitner: Discoverer of Nuclear Fission.*
Greensboro, NC: Morgan Reynolds, Inc., 2000.

Bernstein, Jeremy. *Albert Einstein and the Frontiers of Physics.*
New York: Oxford University Press, 1996.

Burton, Jane, and Taylor, Kim. *The Nature and Science of Energy.*
Milwaukee, WI: Gareth Stevens Publishing, 1998.

Hampton, Wilborn. *Meltdown: A Race Against Nuclear Disaster
At Three Mile Island.* Cambridge, MA: Candlewick Press, 2000.

Parker, Steve. *Electricity.* New York: Dorling Kindersley, 1995.

Richardson, *Hazel. How to Split the Atom.*
New York: Oxford University Press, 1999.

Other Media

The American Experience: Meltdown at Three Mile Island.
VHS. PBS Home Video, 1999.

Modern Marvels: The Manhattan Project.
DVD. The History Channel, 2004.

To learn more about nuclear energy, go to
http://www.nei.org/scienceclub/index.html

INDEX

ABOUT THE AUTHOR

Kathleen Manatt is a long-time writer, editor, and publisher of books for children. Many of her books have been about faraway places, which she likes to visit. She grew up in Illinois, Iowa, New Jersey, and California, and lived in Chicago for many years as an adult. She has climbed pyramids in Mexico, ridden elephants in Thailand, and toured the fjords of Norway. She has also visited Moscow, Lisbon, Paris, Geneva, London, Madrid, Edinburgh, and Barcelona. She now lives in Austin, Texas.

DATE DUE

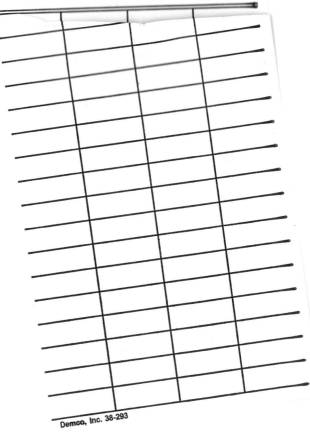